ADAM HAMILTON

Enough
REVISED EDITION
Discovering Joy Through Simplicity and Generosity

Stewardship Program Guide
with Campaign Resources Download

Abingdon Press / Nashville

ENOUGH
STEWARDSHIP PROGRAM GUIDE

Copyright © 2009, 2018
by Abingdon Press
All rights reserved.

No part of this work may be reproduced or transmitted in any form or by any means, electronic or mechanical, including photocopying and recording, or by any information storage or retrieval system, except as may be expressly permitted by the 1976 Copyright Act, the 1998 Digital Millennium Copyright Act, or in writing from the publisher. Requests for permission can be addressed to Rights and Permissions, The United Methodist Publishing House, 810 12th Avenue South, Nashville, TN 37203-4704 or e-mailed to permissions@abingdonpress.com.

ISBN 978-1-7910-2936-4

All Scripture quotations unless noted otherwise are taken from the New Revised Standard Version Bible, copyright © 1989 National Council of the Churches of Christ in the United States of America. Used by permission. All rights reserved worldwide. http://nrsvbibles.org/

Scripture quotations marked (NIV) are taken from the Holy Bible, New International Version®, NIV®. Copyright © 1973, 1978, 1984, 2011 by Biblica, Inc.™ Used by permission of Zondervan. All rights reserved worldwide. www.zondervan.com The "NIV" and "New International Version" are trademarks registered in the United States Patent and Trademark Office by Biblica, Inc.™

MANUFACTURED IN THE UNITED STATES OF AMERICA

STEWARDSHIP PROGRAM GUIDE

CONTENTS

Introduction 7
Program Background 8

1. **Planning** 11
   How to Use the Stewardship Campaign in Your Church 13
   Applying Best Practices with Multilevel Communication 15
   Suggested Communication Target Levels 17
   Thank-You and Recognition Gifts 19
   Stewardship Campaign Schedule Overview 20
   Campaign To-Do List 22

2. **Implementation** 23
   Introduction 25
   Tasks and Resources by Month and Week 26

3. **Communication Resources** 31
   Introduction 33
   Church Newsletter Article 34
   Bulletin Articles 1–6 36
   Mailings 1–5C 40
   E-mail from Pastor 1–6 54
   Bulletin Inserts 1–4 57
   Stewardship Campaign Follow-up 62

4. **Art Resources** 65
   Art Resources for Promoting Your Stewardship Campaign 67

5. **Worship Helps** 73
   Sermon Outlines 1-4 75
   Worship Video Text 90

6. **Small Group Study** 91
   Involving the Congregation in Study 93
   Overview of Small Group Study 94

ACCESS THE CAMPAIGN RESOURCES
DOWNLOAD AT:

AbingdonPress.com/Enough

CAMPAIGN RESOURCES DOWNLOAD

CONTENTS

1 Read Me file

2 Planning and Implementation
   Schedule Overview
   Tasks and Resources
   To-Do List

3 Communication Resources
   Church Newsletter Article
   Bulletin Articles
   Mailings
   E-mails from Pastor
   Bulletin Inserts
   Stewardship Campaign Follow-up

4 Art Resources
   High Resolution for Print
      Covers
      Logos
      Other Graphics
   Low Resolution for Web

5 Worship Helps
   Presentation Images
   Sermon Outlines
   Worship Videos

SIMPLE GIFTS
by Elder Joseph Brackett, 1848

'Tis the gift to be simple, 'tis the gift to be free,
'Tis the gift to come down where we ought to be,
And when we find ourselves in the place just right,
'Twill be in the valley of love and delight.

When true simplicity is gain'd,
To bow and to bend we shan't be asham'd,
To turn, turn will be our delight,
Till by turning, turning we come out right.

INTRODUCTION

One thing has generally been true about stewardship campaigns: Nobody really looks forward to them. In fact, whether it's a big church or a small one, pastors, staff, and church members tend to approach these campaigns as a necessary but unpleasant task. Finance committee members often wish they didn't have to ask for money; members of the congregation often would rather not receive those same pledge cards in the mail, year after year.

This program—*Enough: Discovering Joy Through Simplicity and Generosity*—is based on the experience of The United Methodist Church of the Resurrection in the Kansas City area, as well as on churches' shared experience with stewardship campaigns. You'll find Adam Hamilton's story of how the program came to be in the next section, "Program Background," including the program's roots, philosophy, immediate results, and lasting results.

This campaign, instead of simply asking for money, helps people focus on the blessings they have received from God and how to use their finances to enjoy the fulfilled life that God intends for all of us. As a result, you'll probably find that *Enough* is different from most stewardship campaigns in your experience.

This Stewardship Program Guide is designed to help you plan and carry out a successful campaign. Whether your congregation has two thousand active members or fewer than two hundred, the step-by-step approach and accompanying resources in this guide will help make your task easier. We invite you to use or adapt these materials to the special circumstances of your congregation.

In this guide, you'll find recommendations for:

- planning the program;
- implementation: detailed list of tasks and resources by month and week;
- communication resources: a church newsletter article, bulletin articles, mailings, e-mails from the pastor, bulletin inserts, and a script for follow-up phone calls;
- art resources: images for print and the web;
- worship helps: sermon outlines, worship video descriptions;
- small group study: information about how to organize and lead the small group study that is part of the program.

The guide comes with a download containing electronic files for planning and implementation, communication resources, art resources, and worship helps, so you can tailor the files to the needs of your church setting. The download can be accessed at AbingdonPress.com/Enough.

Blessings to you and your congregation as you experience *Enough: Discovering Joy Through Simplicity and Generosity*!

PROGRAM BACKGROUND

IN 2007, we were preparing our standard stewardship campaign at The United Methodist Church of the Resurrection. The campaign was a time when we celebrated what God had done in the past year, cast a vision for where God was leading our congregation in the future, and sought to inspire people about the biblical concepts of tithing and stewardship.

The format of that standard campaign would seem very familiar to most pastors and staff. In it, we taught about tithing, generosity, and stewardship. I typically would preach two sermons during the campaign, and we showed video testimonials of people who had grown to become tithers. We included print pieces and highlighted the accomplishments of the previous year and the visions we would be pursuing in the coming year. We encouraged everyone to return their commitment cards and had a follow-up phase for those who did not turn in their cards.

Even at its most inspiring, our standard campaign would see attendance drop significantly during the two- to three-week period. More alarmingly, we experienced a steady decline in the percentage of our members turning in commitment cards each year. (The amount of overall giving was increasing, but the number of people returning cards was decreasing, a trend seen in many churches across the country.)

Why We Decided to Take a Different Approach

As we planned our campaign in 2007, one thing became painfully obvious. Many people in our congregation were struggling financially—not because they weren't making enough money, but because they were living beyond their means and were saving nothing.

My team and I began to feel that, instead of launching a traditional stewardship campaign, we needed to help people redefine their relationship with money and start to think carefully and biblically about where we find real joy and what our lives are really about. We needed to acknowledge the problems Americans have in our relationship with money: overspending, maxed-out credit cards, plummeting savings rates, and a lifestyle that is unsustainable. We also knew that we still needed to invite people to make their financial commitments and to speak about giving, but we would talk about this as just one of several important components to a healthy and biblical approach to money. This new approach was based on the belief that our lives are meant to be characterized by simplicity and generosity, and both of these lead to joy.

So we decided to scrap the traditional campaign we had planned. We felt that what was needed was not a fund-raising campaign, but a series of sermons and a campaign that was more pastoral in nature. After prayerful thought and planning, we launched a sermon series called Simplicity, Generosity, and Joy.

Rather than a tone of chastisement, the series incorporated confession and a desire to help. The messages from that sermon series, along with some additional material, later became the initial edition of the book and accompanying video study titled *Enough: Discovering Joy Through Simplicity and Generosity.*

How We Went About It

As we planned the sermon series, we first needed to define the problem and ask, "What are people struggling with? What are the missteps we have made?" I interviewed consumer credit counselors who regularly worked with people in our community. They talked with us about the problems they saw every week and the solutions they offered to their clients.

I sent out an invitation letter to our entire congregation that simply said, "We have a problem: Most of us are struggling in the area of finances, and we are going to try to find wisdom and help you discover joy through simplicity and generosity." The level of response was gratifying.

Then, based on what we had learned from counselors and our congregation, we wrote the sermon series.

We began to teach and to inspire with stories of what a simpler life leading to financial health would look like. Each week, we gave the people tools. One week, we handed out a list of six key financial principles. Another week, we provided a prayer of contentment. We also used bulletin inserts that offered basic tools for making good and prudent financial decisions, including a basic budget worksheet and a life and financial goals questionnaire. To make even more help available, we began a series of financial management workshops that were open to the congregation and the community.

Immediate Results

During our standard stewardship campaign, attendance would drop by about 15 percent. Often, our less committed people would stay away during this time. However, during the new series we saw something very different: attendance swelled! People invited their friends. Those in the community sensed that the series was something they needed. The campaign clearly had struck a chord. Those who attended wanted to find help. They sought a simpler, more financially healthy life that would bring them joy. As attendance grew, we realized we were on the right track.

In the end, the results of the new campaign were dramatic. With the old campaign, our percentage of members returning commitment cards had been 56 percent. That disappointing result made some in the congregation question whether we should ask for commitment cards at all. But I felt that commitment cards are important. They lead people to consider their giving for the coming year. And persons who fill out a commitment card have, in our experience, been more likely to meet this commitment than those who made a commitment but never wrote it down.

In contrast, by the end of the new campaign we had a larger number of members return pledge cards than ever before. Our total pledged giving was up 10 percent. Individuals increased their giving significantly. People shared how the series was life-changing for them as it redefined their goals and finances. And the percentage of individuals and families who returned a commitment card rose from 56 percent to 64 percent.

Perhaps most surprising of all was the congregation's faithfulness in giving. In a typical year we anticipate receiving 92.5 percent of what was actually pledged by our members. We build our budget upon this number, plus another 18 percent from nonpledged giving. In 2008, even after an economic downturn, we received over 97 percent of what was pledged by our members, and this amount, combined with nonpledged giving, led to a significant surplus over budget. (This surplus helped sustain us in 2009 as the economy continued to falter.)

As exciting as that result was, the emphasis was not about increasing our budget. It was about helping people experience the life that God offers and helping them have the kind of relationship with their money that God wants for them. And, as people experienced these changes, they simplified their lives and found greater joy.

Lasting Results

The work we did together as a congregation continues to be reflected in our people, their lives, and their giving patterns. After that first campaign, we increased the number of financial management workshops offered to members and the community. In cooperation with Dave Ramsey and Financial Peace University, we distributed audio CDs to thousands of families, and hundreds of people have taken that course. In addition, we have offered other courses and mentoring from financial experts in our own congregation. It's been a time of ongoing learning and change.

Our hope and prayer is that our experience will inspire and instruct your congregation toward similar results. As you use this churchwide stewardship program involving small group study and congregational worship, our desire is that your entire congregation will be blessed, while individuals and families grow in faith and discover true joy through simplicity and generosity.

— **Adam Hamilton**

CHAPTER ONE

PLANNING

HOW TO USE THE STEWARDSHIP CAMPAIGN IN YOUR CHURCH

The *Enough* stewardship campaign is designed to meet the needs of churches of every size and description. The key to a successful campaign is tailoring the campaign and campaign materials to meet the specific needs of your congregation.

Timing

We recommend a fall campaign so that stewardship commitments are made prior to the start of the new year. The campaign itself is structured to last approximately eight weeks, with planning and follow-up taking place before and after those eight weeks. However, you can abbreviate or extend this time frame as desired. For example, you could shorten the schedule from eight to six weeks by eliminating the introductory small group study session and having only one Consecration Sunday. Or you might extend it by adding a two-week prayer emphasis prior to the campaign kickoff. Again, feel free to adapt the program to fit your schedule and situation. Also, remember to allow plenty of time for any specific items such as commitment cards, bookmarks, giving guide, or signage that you may want designed and/or printed for your campaign.

Tailoring the Campaign to Your Needs

You can make the campaign as elaborate or as simple as desired. This stewardship program guide and the accompanying download include a number of resources you can use, based on your needs and capabilities—from letters and e-mails to sermon outlines created by Adam Hamilton. If you choose, you may simply personalize the letters and other communication tools (noting all prompts within brackets) and reproduce them on your own church letterhead. Or, if resources and time permit, you may use the art provided to create your own custom-made campaign stationery and other creative communications, including posters and worship banners. You may want to use e-mail and your church website, or you might prefer a "print only" campaign. For any items that you may want designed and/or printed for your campaign, make sure to provide sufficient time to produce them before their first planned usage.

Responsibilities

Even the process of planning and implementing the campaign can be tailored to meet your particular needs. For example, you might choose for the pastor(s) and administrative staff to oversee planning and implementation, or you could involve various teams in these responsibilities, such as a stewardship team, worship team, prayer team, small group and study team, communication team, art and design team, or video team (if you want to create your own promotional videos and personal testimonials). Again, the key is to make it your own. You know best what will meet the needs of your congregation.

APPLYING BEST PRACTICES WITH MULTILEVEL COMMUNICATION

IN this book *Creating a Climate for Giving*, Donald Joiner says there are benefits of using a multilevel approach in communicating with different people (Discipleship Resources, 2002). Wayne Garrett and Dan Dick, both authors on this topic, also support this concept. They acknowledge that different people hear the same information differently. Communicating differently to different people within the congregation according to their commitment levels results in:

- spiritual growth
- discipleship growth
- financial growth
- congregational growth

Let's consider some of the ways these areas of growth connect and overlap:

- In congregations with high levels of financial contributions, programs that annually promote estimates of giving result in increased giving. Eugene Grimm states that those who make annual estimates of giving usually give at least 30 percent more than those who do not.[1]

- In congregations that practice annual commitment programs, people give much more than the amount indicated on their commitment cards when they are informed and inspired about ministry and mission needs.

- In congregations where members are taught at different levels of their spiritual journey to grow in their discipleship and stewardship commitment, there is greater spiritual maturity and financial health.

- In congregations where members are connected to small groups, classes, mission projects, and other volunteering programs, there is increased giving of time and finances.

- In congregations where people are informed and excited about what the church is doing year-round, there is increased generosity and joy.

---

[1] Eugene Grimm, *Generous People: How to Encourage Vital Stewardship* (Nashville: Abingdon Press, 1992), 49.

- In congregations that celebrate weekly in worship what God is doing, people give not only to budgets but also to specific ministry and missions opportunities that change lives for Christ.
- In congregations that have the expectation of tithing and proportional giving, there are giving goals that can demonstrate growth in discipleship.
- In congregations that support year-round, biblically based generosity, stewardship, and financial management studies, growth in giving results because of deeper discipleship.

Clearly, there is a relationship between specific, planned, multilevel methods of communicating within the congregation and growth in every area of congregational life.

SUGGESTED COMMUNICATION TARGET LEVELS

When communicating with church members regarding stewardship commitments, you should consider targeting five identifiable levels or groups:

Level 1: Less-than-actives / Lapsed Members

These members have no record of attendance or giving during the past three months. They need multiple letters and contacts. Always use a postage-paid, return envelope if any kind of response is requested. Encourage these members to come back to worship, but don't send them an Estimate of Giving letter.

Level 2: Attenders / Nongivers

These members have attended worship in the last year, but there is no record of their giving. Because they attend but usually do not respond, they need constant repetition of message. The focus in communications to this group should be on the importance of giving to God, giving as an act of worship, steps on getting started, and sensitivity to possible financial issues. (They should receive the Giving Guide, which you'll find in the download.)

Level 3: New Members

These members have joined the church in the last twelve months and are developing their giving patterns. The focus in communications to this group should be on how they can honor God in their giving and make a difference. (They should receive the Giving Guide.)

Level 4: Supporters / Regular Attenders

These members are regular attenders who worship and serve and are involved at an active level of personal and financial commitment. The focus in communications to this group should be to challenge them to step up toward tithing or increasing their percentage of giving if they are not yet experiencing their goals in joyful giving. (They should receive the Giving Guide.)

Level 5: Actives / Lead Donors

Actives are the leaders who are most generous in giving their time, testimony, tithes, and special offerings as a Christian lifestyle. They are the best source for increased giving. The focus in communications to this group should be on personal appreciation, celebration of results, and the joy of generosity. They should receive a personal, handwritten thank-you note. (They should receive the Giving Guide.)

All persons in every level need to hear what a difference their giving makes and how their giving is an act of faithful worship to God.

THANK-YOU AND RECOGNITION GIFTS

Each of the letters for donors and new members provides a place to describe a thank-you gift. At The United Methodist Church of the Resurrection, Adam Hamilton and his team have tried several things. In this series, each person who turned in a commitment card received a coffee mug—even if a card was turned in without a dollar commitment. This small recognition of the community was well received.

A new gift tradition has now been launched at the Church of the Resurrection for new members as a way to encourage and recognize their first commitment. Each new member who turns in a commitment card receives a copy of the *New Interpreter's Study Bible* from the church. It is a more expensive gift, but it honors this first participation and commitment from new members in a significant way and sends a clear message about the importance of the commitment.

STEWARDSHIP CAMPAIGN SCHEDULE OVERVIEW

Here's a quick overview of the stewardship campaign schedule, with one month each for the following program phases: planning, getting started, campaign underway, Consecration and Celebration Sundays, and follow-up. For a more detailed schedule, see "Tasks and Resources by Month and Week," in Chapter 2: Implementation.

Using this schedule will help keep your campaign on track in the coming weeks. If you like, create your own campaign to-do list on the page following this overview.

Planning (Month _____)

- Planning and Budget Review and Approval

- Order copies of *Enough* program components:
  ◊ Book
  ◊ DVD
  ◊ Leader Guide
  ◊ Stewardship Program Guide with Campaign Resources Download

- Review this Stewardship Guide and decide which items may need to be designed and printed. This might include items such as commitment cards, bookmarks, giving guide, signage, and so forth. Sample copy and graphics for many of these items can be found in the Communication Resources and Art Resources folders in the download at AbingdonPress.com/Enough. Be sure to allocate plenty of time to receive the items before your first usage.

- Other: _____

Getting Started (Month _____)

Weeks 1–2: Upload introductory materials to website.

Week 3: Distribute books, DVD, and Leader Guide.

Week 4: Mailing #1 sent out.

Campaign Underway (Month _____)

Week 1: Upload sermon, e-mail, and bulletin article to website. Mailing #2 goes out. Small group study begins with Session 1.

Week 2: Upload sermon, e-mail, bulletin article, and bulletin inserts to website. Small group study continues with Session 2.

Week 3: Upload sermon, e-mail, and bulletin article to website. Small group study continues with Session 3.

Week 4: Upload sermon, e-mail, and pledging tools to website. Mailing #3 goes out. Small group study concludes with Session 4.

Consecration and Celebration Sundays (Month _____)

Week 1: First Consecration Sunday. Distribute additional commitment cards. Distribute thank-you gifts.

Week 2: Second Consecration Sunday. Distribute additional commitment cards.

Week 3: Follow-up calls begin.

Week 4: Celebration Sunday. Share results of the stewardship campaign.

Follow-up (Month _____)

Week 1: Valued member survey mailed to nonresponding members.

CAMPAIGN TO-DO LIST

- [ ] _____
- [ ] _____
- [ ] _____
- [ ] _____
- [ ] _____
- [ ] _____
- [ ] _____
- [ ] _____
- [ ] _____
- [ ] _____
- [ ] _____
- [ ] _____
- [ ] _____
- [ ] _____

CHAPTER TWO

IMPLEMENTATION

INTRODUCTION

After planning the campaign, it's time to get started. To guide you in implementing the campaign, this section gives a detailed, week-by-week schedule, listing tasks to accomplish and resources to use.

All the resources listed in this schedule will be shown in Chapter 3: Communication Resources. Electronic copies of all the resources will be found on the Campaign Resources Download, so they can be edited and tailored to your needs. These include such items as articles, e-mails, inserts, and letters, as well as art and graphics.

Remember that these materials are designed to be customized, and they contain references to resources that you may not have or choose not to use. For example, if your pastor will not use a sermon series during the campaign that follows the outlines offered with this guide, you will need to edit letters and bulletin inserts accordingly. Be sure also to follow prompts in the documents to include church-specific information.

Along with these resources, you may also wish to create your own campaign stationery and other creative communications, such as posters and worship banners.

TASKS AND RESOURCES BY MONTH AND WEEK

August
Weeks 1–2

- Planning and budget review and approval
- Order copies of *Enough* materials: books, DVDs, Leader Guides, Stewardship Program Guide with Campaign Resources Download (allow time for delivery)
- After reviewing the Stewardship Program Guide, decide which items may need to be designed and printed for use with the campaign. These items may include commitment cards, bookmarks, giving guide, signage, and so forth. Sample copy and graphics for many of these items can be found in the Communication Resources and Art Resources folders in the download. Be sure to allocate plenty of time to receive the items before your first usage.

September
Weeks 1–2

- Church Newsletter Article: *Enough* Stewardship Campaign Introduction
- Upload introductory materials to website: *Enough* Stewardship Campaign Introduction, Overview, and Schedule; details regarding small group study opportunities

Week 3
To Do for Sunday

- Distribute books, DVDs, and Leader Guides to small group leaders
- Bulletin Article 1: *Enough: Discovering Joy Through Simplicity and Generosity* (run for three consecutive Sundays)

Week 4
To Do for Sunday

- Bulletin Article 1: *Enough: Discovering Joy Through Simplicity and Generosity* (repeat)
- Small group leaders announce *Enough* study and distribute books to participants (additional groups may meet Monday–Friday)

Week 4
To Do Monday–Friday

- Send Mailing 1: *Enough* Stewardship Campaign Invitation

October

Week 1
To Do for Sunday

- Bulletin Article 1: *Enough: Discovering Joy Through Simplicity and Generosity* (repeat)
- Sermon 1: "When Dreams Become Nightmares"
- Small group Session 1: "When Dreams Become Nightmares" (additional groups may meet Monday–Friday)

Week 1
To Do Monday–Friday

- Upload Sermon 1 to church website
- Send E-mail 1 from pastor
- Mailing 2: Six Key Financial Principles Letter (on Friday)

Week 2
To Do for Sunday

- Bulletin Article 2: Six Key Financial Principles
- Bulletin Insert 1: My Life and Financial Goals Worksheet
- Bulletin Insert 2: Basic Budget Worksheet
- Sermon 2: "Wisdom and Finance"
- Display and announce financial planning books and resources in designated area of church (for loan and/or sale)
- Small group Session 2: "Wisdom and Finance" (additional groups may meet Monday–Friday)

Week 2
To Do Monday–Friday

- Upload Sermon 2, Bulletin Article 2, Bulletin Insert 1, and Bulletin Insert 2 to website
- Send E-mail 2 from pastor

Week 3
To Do for Sunday

- Bulletin Article 3: Contentment Is Key
- Sermon 3: "Cultivating Contentment"
- Small group Session 3: "Cultivating Contentment" (additional groups may meet Monday–Friday)

Week 3
To Do Monday–Friday

- Upload Sermon 3 to church website
- Send E-mail 3 from pastor

Week 4
To Do for Sunday

- Bulletin Article 4: Personal Goals and Commitment
- Bulletin Insert 4: Personal Goals and Commitment
- Sermon 4: "Defined by Generosity"
- Small group Session 4: "Defined by Generosity" (additional groups may meet Monday–Friday)

Week 4
To Do Monday–Friday

- Upload Sermon 4 to website
- Also upload Personal Goals and Commitment, Giving Guide, and Instructions for Online Pledging
- Send E-mail 4 from pastor
- Mailing 3: Estimate of Giving Letters, Giving Guide, Estimate of Giving Commitment Card (see Bulletin Insert 3 for copy that can be used to create your church's cards), and envelope (use first-class postage; must arrive before next Sunday);
Note: if you've chosen to design and print giving guides or commitment cards, this will need to be done in advance of week 4. Make sure to give yourself ample time to receive any printed pieces in advance of the mailing.

November

Week 1
To Do for Sunday (Consecration Sunday #1)

- Bulletin Article 5: Consecration Sunday
- Make available extra Estimate of Giving Commitment Cards

Week 1
To Do Monday–Friday

- Send E-mail 5 from pastor

Week 2
To Do for Sunday (Consecration Sunday #2)

- Bulletin Article 5: Consecration Sunday (repeat)
- Make available extra Estimate of Giving Commitment Cards

Week 2
To Do Monday–Friday

- Send E-mail 6 from pastor
- Send Mailing 4: Follow-up Nonresponder Letter

Week 3
To Do for Sunday

- Bulletin Article 6: Thank You

Week 3
To Do Monday–Friday

- Begin follow-up by staff and laypersons: Caring Contact Calls

Week 4
To Do for Sunday (Celebration Sunday)

- Bulletin insert suggestion: Print your ministry plans for the coming year on a bulletin insert
- Along with celebrating the results of the campaign, set aside time during worship to consecrate these gifts for ministry in the coming year

January

Week 1
To Do Monday–Friday

- Send Mailing 5: Pledge Confirmation / Thank-You Letter and Bookmark to responding members; Valued Member Survey to nonresponding members.
  Note: bookmarks will need to be designed and printed in advance, so make sure to allocate enough time for the bookmarks to be produced for your mailing.

CHAPTER THREE

COMMUNICATION RESOURCES

INTRODUCTION

This section contains copies of all the resources listed in the detailed schedule. Electronic copies of all these resources will also be found on the Campaign Resources Download, so they can be edited and tailored to your needs. (The copies printed in this guide are not intended to be photocopied; instead please use the electronic copies in the download.)

Remember that these materials are designed to be customized, and they contain references to resources that you may not have or choose not to use. For example, if your pastor will not use a sermon series during the campaign that follows the outlines offered with this guide, you will need to edit letters and bulletin inserts accordingly. Be sure also to follow prompts in the documents to include church-specific information.

You may want to have items such as commitment cards and bookmarks designed and printed for use during the campaign. Along with these resources, you may also wish to create your own campaign stationery and other creative communications, such as posters and worship banners. Allow plenty of time to design and print these items before their first usage.

CHURCH NEWSLETTER ARTICLE

ENOUGH STEWARDSHIP CAMPAIGN INTRODUCTION

Enough: Discovering Joy Through Simplicity and Generosity

One of Jesus' great teaching parables involves a sower who cast seed along the ground. The sower hoped the seeds would sprout, grow, and bear good fruit. Some seeds did just that, producing a great harvest. But others, Jesus said, fell among thorns and, though they began to grow, these good plants were quickly choked out. Jesus said the thorns were "the cares of the world and the lure of wealth" (Matthew 13:22).

In a culture where having "enough" seems to have become a never-ending pursuit, Jesus' parable remains incredibly relevant. Many of us are chasing the American dream in ways that lead to stress, anxiety, and fear—thorns that can rob us of the ability to enjoy the abundant lives of purpose that God intended for us.

All of us have struggled with these issues at one time or another. They are important issues that we cannot ignore. This is why, over the next [number] weeks, we will be having a churchwide study and worship emphasis called *Enough: Discovering Joy Through Simplicity and Generosity*. During this time we will explore what the Bible teaches us about financial management through corporate worship and small group study. (Visit [church website address] for details about small group study opportunities.) We'll hear expert advice and stories about what others have learned by working through financial challenges. Each week we will provide you with some practical tools you can use to assess your financial situation and develop a financial plan with a biblical foundation.

At the conclusion of the emphasis, we will have the opportunity to make personal commitments of our offerings to God through our church in the coming year. We will consecrate these commitments in the worship service on two consecutive Sundays. (See the schedule that follows.)

I hope you will join us in the coming weeks as we look at how we can manage our financial resources and truly experience simplicity, generosity, and joy.

Schedule of Events

[Date] "When Dreams Become Nightmares"
[Date] "Wisdom and Finance"
[Date] "Cultivating Contentment"
[Date] "Defined by Generosity"

[Date] Small Group Study Ends
[Date] Consecration Sunday 1
[Date] Consecration Sunday 2
[Date] Celebration Sunday

BULLETIN ARTICLE 1

Enough: Discovering Joy Through Simplicity and Generosity

ON Sunday, [date], we will begin a churchwide study and worship emphasis called *Enough: Discovering Joy Through Simplicity and Generosity*. Over a period of [number] weeks, we will look at some of the financial challenges facing us as a nation and examine our own spending, saving, and giving habits. In addition to exploring biblical principles of financial management, we will learn ways to assess our financial situation and develop a financial plan that will allow us to experience the true joy that comes through simplicity and generosity.

At the end of the emphasis, we will have the opportunity to make personal commitments of giving for the coming year. We will consecrate these commitments on Sunday, [date], and Sunday, [date]. Visit our website [website address] for more information, including details about small group study opportunities during this time.

BULLETIN ARTICLE 2

Six Key Financial Principles

Today in worship we will look closely at biblical principles of money management and learn how they apply to our daily lives. We will review some common pitfalls and cultural traps and discover how to avoid them. We also will learn about the Six Key Financial Principles, which are summarized below.

We hope you will take time this week to read these principles and Scriptures. They will make a great table devotional for you and your family. By practicing these biblical principles, all of us can find greater simplicity, contentment, generosity, and joy for our lives. Also, be sure to check out the financial management resources on display today in [location].

1. **Put God first in your living and giving. (2 Corinthians 9:6-7)**
   Put God first in your living and your giving. Give your tithe and offering from the "top" of your paycheck, and then live on whatever remains.

2. **Prepare a spending plan and track all expenses monthly. (Proverbs 27:23-24)**
   Creating a budget means developing a plan in which you tell your money what you want it to do. Tracking your expenses is like getting on the scales to see how you are doing.

3. **Simplify your lifestyle; live below your means. (Matthew 6:19-33)**
   Because this discipline is critical to the success of any financial plan, next Sunday's sermon will be devoted to this topic.

4. **Provide immediately for an emergency fund. (1 Timothy 6:9-12)**
   An emergency fund is an account separate from checking or long-term savings that is set aside specifically for emergencies.

5. **Pay off all credit card debt; use cash or debit cards, not credit cards. (Proverbs 22:7)**
   As you are building your emergency fund, begin to pay off your credit card debt and start using cash or debit cards for purchases. If you must use a credit card, be sure to pay off the debt monthly.

6. **Practice long-range saving and investing habits. (Luke 14:28)**
   Saving money is the Number 1 wise money management principle everyone should practice. There are three types of savings we should have: emergency savings, savings for wants and goals, and retirement savings.

BULLETIN ARTICLE 3

Contentment Is Key

DO you have a tough time separating "wants" from "needs"? Do you sometimes feel consumed by the desire to have more? Do you ever look at your surroundings and feel overwhelmed by the sheer volume of things? When is enough, enough?

Today in worship, we will release these burdens, address our human tendencies head-on, and learn how to change our ways.

BULLETIN ARTICLE 4

Personal Goals and Commitment

What defines your life? Is it wealth? belongings? faith? Many of us live with a scarcity mentality, worried that we must gather and hoard as much as possible, saving for some imagined "rainy day." Others go to the opposite extreme, focusing on self-gratification. But the Bible promises both God's blessings and joy for those who choose to live another way.

During today's service, we will take action to change our lives by setting five specific personal goals to work toward over the next year. You'll find in this bulletin a Personal Goals and Commitment Card. Take it home and place it in your Bible for your personal reference in the coming year.

Note that one of these five commitments is your estimate of giving for the coming year. This week, you will be receiving an Estimate of Giving Commitment Card in the mail. On a practical level, we ask our members to turn in estimate of giving commitment cards each year so that our Finance Committee is able to set an accurate ministry budget for the coming year. This allows us to make the most of every dollar given to the church. On a personal level, the commitment card is an opportunity for you to spend time in prayer and reflection, considering what offering you will make to God through our church in the coming year. Please be watching for the mailing; then fill out the card and bring it with you to worship next Sunday. You also can pledge online at [website address].

BULLETIN ARTICLE 5

Consecration Sunday

Today is Consecration Sunday. In our worship service, we will have the opportunity to consecrate our personal commitments for the coming year. You should have received an Estimate of Giving Commitment Card in the mail. If you did not receive one, or if you forgot to bring it with you today, additional cards are available in [location]. We invite you to prayerfully consider what your offering to God through our church will be in the coming year. Then fill out a card and bring it forward at the conclusion of the worship service.

BULLETIN ARTICLE 6

Thank You

Over the past few weeks, we've been looking at what the Bible teaches us about financial management. We've considered how we make and spend money, how we deal with debt, and how we save and invest for the future. We've examined how God wants us to relate to our money and earthly possessions, and we've explored what it means to live a life of gratitude and contentment. We have studied and worshiped . . . and we have responded!

On two Consecration Sundays, we received more than [number] personal commitments for the coming year. Thank you for prayerfully considering what offering you will make to God through our church in the coming year. Your gifts are an act of worship and an investment in opportunities for God to work through us. Our prayer is that you will find greater contentment and simplicity in your life as you put God first in your giving and your living. May we all experience the joy that comes from knowing that our gifts honor God and change lives!

MAILING 1

ENOUGH STEWARDSHIP CAMPAIGN INVITATION

Dear Friends,

I really hope that you will join me in worship in the coming weeks for a churchwide study and worship emphasis titled *Enough: Discovering Joy Through Simplicity and Generosity*. We live in a society that tells us "you deserve it now," whether or not we can afford it or really even need it.

I'm sure we've all struggled with these issues at one time or another. I know that I have. Beginning next weekend, we are going to explore what the Bible teaches us about financial management. We'll look at what others have learned by working through financial challenges. Each week I'll be providing you with some tools you can use to assess your financial situation and develop a financial plan with a biblical foundation.

These are important issues that we cannot ignore. I hope you will join me as we look at how we can manage our financial resources and truly experience that God is "Enough."

In Christ,

Communication Resources

MAILING 2

SIX KEY FINANCIAL PRINCIPLES LETTER

[Date]

Dear [church name] member,

Last Sunday our congregation learned about the Six Key Financial Principles, and we are enclosing another copy of the principles to emphasize their importance. Please read these principles and Scriptures as a family. By practicing these biblical principles, all of us can find greater simplicity, contentment, generosity, and joy for our lives.

Our church would like to help you with this part of your spiritual life in the coming year. We will offer Sunday morning classes and small group opportunities designed to help you with your finances. Please visit our website at [website address] to register or request more information about these study opportunities. With God's help, everyone can save more and give more by eliminating waste and reducing debt.

On Sunday, [date], the sermon will be titled "Cultivating Contentment." We live in a society full of economic problems that result from materialism. This message will offer practical and biblical help for the financial issues that challenge and stress so many of us. In Matthew 6:19-20, 24 (NIV) we read these words: "Do not store up for yourselves treasures on earth. . . . But store up for yourselves treasures in heaven. . . . You cannot serve both God and money." You will hear a message on how to declutter your life, work toward developing contentment, and learn God's will for our lives in the area of finances.

On Sunday, [date], we will have the final message in this sermon series, titled "Defined by Generosity." We will be distributing commitment cards for you to record your personal commitment for the coming year. The following Sunday, [date], will be our first Consecration Sunday. In worship we will bring our commitment cards forward and consecrate our personal commitments. We will have a second Consecration Sunday on [date] to ensure that everyone has the chance to participate in this meaningful service.

This year more than [number] households returned a commitment card as a witness of giving to God and as a way to plan their giving for our ministry. We hope and pray to increase the number of households that will take a step out in faith and return a commitment card for God's ministry and mission at our church in [next calendar year].

Join us in worship as we celebrate and consecrate our gifts to the ministry of this church in the coming year. We can live as people of hope, learning how to live with simplicity, contentment, generosity, and true joy!

In Christ,

MAILING 3

ESTIMATE OF GIVING LETTERS*

INSTRUCTIONS

This mailing should be sent after the fourth Sunday of the campaign ("Defined by Generosity") and before the first Consecration Sunday. The mailing includes three important components, all of which are provided on the following pages and in the download:

- a letter tailored to each of four groups: actives / lead donors, supporters / regular attenders, new members, and attenders / nongivers;

- a Giving Guide, which helps each household think through the reasons to give, expectations, and benefits of turning in a commitment card; and

- a commitment card (see Bulletin Insert 3 for copy).

---

*Note: some churches may choose to design the Giving Guide and commitment cards which will be used in this mailing. If your church chooses to do so, artwork provided in the Art Resources folder may be useful. Make sure to allocate sufficient time to design and print the piece in advance of their first usage.

Communication Resources

MAILING 3A

ESTIMATE OF GIVING LETTER FOR ACTIVES / LEAD DONORS

[Date]

Dear [church name] member [or personalize],

I'm writing this letter to those members who last year were among our top [number] donors to say thank you. Together, you are responsible for [dollar amount] of our giving in [current calendar year], and without your support, our church's ministry could not happen.

Thanks to you, we've welcomed over [number] children, youth, and adults into church membership in [current calendar year]. Your offerings helped us teach more than [number] children in Sunday school and other children's programs. You helped us minister to more than [number] teenagers. You enabled us to provide missions support through our denomination and our mission partners here in [city / community]; you allowed us to offer pastoral care and discipleship ministries to more than [number] adults, and so much more.

I am guessing that many of you receiving this letter are already giving 10 percent of your income—the biblical tithe. Some of you already give more than a tithe. To you I simply want to say, "Great job!" This is a milestone and an expression of your faith. If you are not yet tithing, I'd like to invite you to take a step in that direction. You've already shown yourself to be a generous giver. You might look to see what it would take to begin tithing. If you can't take the step all in one year, try increasing your giving by 1 percent each year.

For me [and spouse's name, if applicable], tithing is one of the great blessings in life. Some years ago, I/we began stretching beyond the tithe, and that too has been a meaningful part of my/our life. Each spring as I/we prepare my/our income and giving statements for income tax preparation, I/we find great joy in knowing that I/we gave God my/our tithes and offerings.

Enclosed you will find a Giving Guide that can help you as you consider your commitment for [next calendar year], an Estimate of Giving Commitment Card, and an envelope. This Sunday, [date], we'll be returning the commitment cards at the end of the worship service. Please take a few minutes to pray about your giving for next year. Then fill out your card and bring it with you to worship this weekend. (You may want to consider the option for automatic giving. That will help you avoid falling behind in your giving. It also will help the church by ensuring that whether you are in town or out of town, your offerings will continue.) If you would rather fill out your card online, you can do so by going to [website address].

Again, thank you for all that you do to make possible the ministry of this church. You make a difference here!

In Christ,

P.S. Be sure to stop by this weekend, after you've turned in your Estimate of Giving Commitment Card, to pick up your [gift item]—our way of saying thank you for turning in your card.

MAILING 3B

ESTIMATE OF GIVING LETTER FOR SUPPORTERS / REGULAR ATTENDERS

[Date]

Dear [church name] member,

This Sunday, [date], is the time we ask our members to return their [next calendar year] Estimate of Giving Commitment Cards as we make plans for our ministry for the coming year. It will be a great and inspiring weekend in worship, and we'll be giving each household that returns their estimate of giving commitment card a [gift item] as an expression of thanks for your continued support of the ministry.

I want to remind you why we ask our members to turn in Estimate of Giving Commitment Cards each year, and to offer a specific invitation to you.

On a very practical level, we ask you to turn in an Estimate of Giving Commitment Card so our Finance Committee will be able to set an accurate ministry budget for the coming year, making the most of every gift. On a personal level, the return of the Estimate of Giving Commitment Card invites you to spend time in prayer and reflection, considering what your offerings should be for the coming year. I [and spouse's name, if applicable] look at what my/our expected income is going to be in the coming year, and I/we revise my/our giving based upon that figure. I/We give the first 10 percent of my/our income to the church as a tithe. Above that, I/we give other offerings to the church and to various charities and mission projects.

You may already practice tithing—giving 10 percent. If you do, I want to commend you. If you are not yet tithing, I'd like to invite you to consider taking a step toward tithing this year. Take a look at your current giving, determine what percentage of your income you are currently giving as an offering to God, and consider raising that amount by at least 1 percentage point. This is how most people begin to tithe—by gradually increasing their giving until they hit the goal.

We are grateful for your financial support of the church. Your giving this year has made a difference in the lives of children, youth, and adults in our church, as well as in the lives of people everywhere we have been in mission and ministry in the world.

Enclosed you will find a Giving Guide that can help you as you consider your commitment for [next calendar year], an Estimate of Giving Commitment Card, and an envelope. Please pray about your giving, and take a moment to reflect upon what offering you would make to God through our church in the coming year. Then bring the card with you to worship this weekend. You also can pledge online at [website address].

Again, thank you for your support of God's work here at [church name]!

In Christ,

MAILING 3C

ESTIMATE OF GIVING LETTER FOR NEW MEMBERS

[Date]

Dear [church name] member,

　I'm writing to each of our members who joined this year to let you know that this Sunday, [date], is the time when we invite every member to return their Estimate of Giving Commitment Card for [next calendar year]. There are two reasons we ask each member to fill out and return these cards each year. First, this allows the church to accurately plan our ministries for the coming year, developing our ministry budget based upon what our members tell us they plan to give. Second, the act of filling out a card is a way of inviting each member to prayerfully set a goal for giving for the coming year.

　For me [and spouse's name, if applicable], this is an important decision each year, and one that I/we make as an expression of my/our faith and commitment to Christ and an investment in the work of the church. I/We know that my/our giving is a way of furthering the mission and vision of the church. By means of our giving—yours and mine/ours—[number] new people have joined the church so far this year, many of whom have made a new or renewed commitment to Christ. By our offerings we have helped more than [number] children and over [number] teenagers grow in their faith. Through our offerings we provided pastoral care, nursing home visits, discipleship opportunities, and hundreds of other ministries in the church. And by our offerings we provided over [dollar amount] to mission causes outside the walls of our church.

　I am including three items in this envelope: a Giving Guide that can help you as you consider your commitment for [next calendar year], an Estimate of Giving Commitment Card, and an envelope. I invite you to pray about the commitment you would make to Christ for the coming year and then bring your card with you to worship this weekend. As a small token of our thanks, we'll be giving a [gift item] to each family that returns their card.

　My hope and prayer is that your giving is a source of blessing and joy in your life.

In Christ,

MAILING 3D

ESTIMATE OF GIVING LETTER FOR ATTENDERS / NONGIVERS

[Date]

Dear [church name] member,

This Sunday, [date], is the time when we invite each member household to return a commitment card to the church sharing their financial commitment for the coming year. Our records indicate that you have not given during this current year, and for that reason I wanted to touch base with you and give you a special invitation.

Some receiving this letter are planning to give in December, and if that group includes you, I want to thank you in advance for your gift.

Some receiving this letter are struggling financially and not in a position to give. My word to you is simply that we care, and if there is any way we can be of support to you—by praying with or for you, talking with you, or providing other help—please contact us at [phone number].

Some receiving this letter may not have given this year because of some disappointment with the church. If there is any place where we have missed the mark, we'd like to know by receiving a note using the enclosed postage-paid envelope. Our hope is to be a blessing in your life, and we'd like a chance to improve our ministry.

I [and spouse's name, if applicable] give to the Lord for several reasons. I/We give as an expression of thanks and praise to God for the blessings in my/our life/lives. I/We give because I/we want to help support God's work through our church. And I/we give because, in the Scriptures, God asks us to give. I/We give to a host of other causes, but my/our first offerings—my/our tithe—goes to the church to honor God and support the work of the ministry. I am/We are blessed and feel joy in honoring God in this way.

For the coming year, if you are able, I'd like to invite you to make a pledge of some kind, giving an amount that you feel in your heart God would have you give. I think you will find that you are blessed by your giving. Enclosed you will find a Giving Guide that can help you as you consider your commitment, along with an Estimate of Giving Commitment Card. Please return your card on Sunday, [date]. We need to hear from every active member, regardless of the amount of his or her estimate of giving. Even if you can't give or choose not to give, please let us know this. This will save us on follow-up contacts and letters.

I am grateful that you are a member of the church and wish you God's blessings in the coming year!

In Christ,

MAILING 3E

GIVING GUIDE (TO GO WITH ALL ESTIMATE OF GIVING LETTERS)*

Giving Guide

This year we invite you to celebrate the joy of generosity as you offer your Estimate of Giving Commitment Card for [next calendar year]. We encourage you to find greater contentment and simplicity in your lives as you put God first in your giving and living and to experience the joy that comes from knowing our gifts honor God and change lives. Our challenge as members is to find ways to grow deeper in our faith. One way to do this is to offer our financial blessings to God through our tithes and offerings. Through these gifts, we invest in God's vision and purpose and create an opportunity for God to work through us. Our gifts to God each week are an act of worship; and our offerings are vitally necessary to change lives, transform communities, and renew mainline churches.

Why is giving important?

The Bible has much to say about wisdom and finances, with 2,300 verses that tell us to be generous and good stewards of our resources. Jesus taught generosity and sacrifice. He demanded that his followers serve not wealth but God, and in the parable of the talents he taught that God will hold us each accountable for what we do with all our earthly possessions.

What is expected of me?

The Bible teaches us to give a tithe, or the first 10 percent of what we earn, to God and the church's work. For some, giving 10 percent is a very difficult goal. For others, it is the starting point, and their giving far exceeds 10 percent. The important thing is that you start somewhere, that your giving be in proportion to your income, that your giving reflects an appropriate offering to God given your means, and that your offerings express both your desire to serve the Lord and your investment in God's work.

Begin by determining what percentage of your income you are giving to God. If you are not yet tithing, consider taking a step toward tithing this year. For example, if you now give 3 percent of your income, consider increasing your gift to 4 percent, and add 1 percent each year until you reach the tithing goal.

Our prayer is that everyone will grow in his or her faith through giving financially to the ministries of the church and experience the joy and blessings that come from financial generosity.

Everything we have belongs to God.

> *"A tithe [tenth] of everything from the land, whether grain from the soil or fruit from the trees, belongs to the Lord; it is holy to the Lord."*
>
> *(Leviticus 27:30 NIV)*

---

*Note: some churches may choose to design the Giving Guide as brochure rather than a letter. If your church chooses to do so, artwork provided in the Art Resources folder may be useful. Make sure to allocate sufficient time to design and print the piece in advance of its first usage.

Why do I need to return an Estimate of Giving Commitment Card?

There are two reasons why it is important that every member of our church family return an Estimate of Giving Commitment Card. First, the process of prayerfully asking God to guide your decision and then making a commitment to serve the Lord with your financial gifts is an act of worship, an expression of gratitude and praise to God. Second, on a more practical note, your commitment allows our church to budget and better plan for our ministries, key objectives, and mission outreach programs.

What if financial hardship prohibits me from making a commitment this year?

Don't let your inability to give at this time keep you from worship. Remember that God honors your faithfulness and that your acceptance at [church name] is not based on your capacity to give. We ask that everyone return an Estimate of Giving Commitment Card even if it is a limited financial commitment at this time. You can always increase or decrease your commitment if your situation changes by calling the church. Also, be sure to let our pastoral staff know of your situation so that they can pray for and support you during any difficulty. We also offer classes to assist members in becoming better managers of all that God gives them. For information, call [name] at [number] or e-mail [email address].

We reap what we sow.

> *"The point is this: the one who sows sparingly will also reap sparingly, and the one who sows bountifully will also reap bountifully."*
>
> *(2 Corinthians 9:6)*

Why do I need to turn in a new commitment card each year?

Financial situations change from year to year, and if we are growing in our faith, our annual commitment should likewise reflect that giving growth. Each year, our church budget is based on the growing commitments of our congregation.

Should I use electronic funds transfer?

Electronic funds transfer (EFT) is the easiest, most cost-effective giving option for both you and the church. With EFT, you can reinforce your commitment to give your tithes and offerings to God first, before anything else. Taking that one easy step each year guarantees that the church will receive your gifts on a regular basis, even if you are out of town or forget one week. And on a practical note, EFT reduces the need for additional staff to process offerings. If you choose this option, you must return an Estimate of Giving Commitment Card each year authorizing the electronic funds transfer. Complete the EFT information and attach a voided check for the account you will use. For more information contact us at [phone number].

To whom much has been given . . .

> *"From everyone who has been given much, much will be demanded; and from the one who has been entrusted with much, much more will be asked."*
>
> *(Luke 12:48 NIV)*

MAILING 4

FOLLOW-UP NONRESPONDER LETTER

[Date]

Dear [church name] member,

As pastor of [church name], I get to hear story after story of how our church is changing lives, transforming our community, and renewing other churches. Your support makes ministry possible.

I am writing to all members who have yet to return their annual stewardship Estimate of Giving Commitment Cards to encourage you to return your card as soon as possible. Receiving your [next calendar year] estimate of giving helps make it possible for us to budget, plan, and provide appropriate resources for our ministries. I am grateful for so many who support ministry at [church name], and I invite you to join us by returning your Estimate of Giving Commitment Card.

My hope is that this commitment will also be an important step in your faith. Generosity is a personal act of worship in which we express our gratitude to God and experience God's blessings and joy.

Whenever I send a letter like this, I am aware that some families are facing difficult financial times. If your finances are uncertain, a 10 percent tithe may not be possible. So, I encourage you to estimate whatever percentage you realistically think you will be able to contribute in support of the church's ministries. As your situation changes throughout the year, you can easily adjust your estimate of giving up or down with a phone call or e-mail.

You may return your Estimate of Giving Commitment Card in the offering this Sunday, or send it to the church by mail. Alternatively, you may choose to make your commitment online at [website address].

If you are receiving this letter and have already returned your card, please let us know by calling [name] at [phone number].

I am so grateful for you and how you make the ministries of the church possible. Please feel free to call me at [phone number] if you have any questions. I'll see you in worship this weekend!

In Christ,

MAILING 5A

PLEDGE CONFIRMATION / THANK-YOU LETTER

[Date]

Dear [name],

Thank you for sharing your estimate of giving with our church this year. You are an important part of the ministry of [church name] and of God's work in our community and the world. Through your gifts, you will be a part of changing the lives of children and youth, ministering to those in need, and welcoming others into the embrace of Christ.

Over the past few weeks, we've been looking at how we relate to our earthly possessions, how we make money and spend it, how we deal with debt, and how we live a life of gratitude no matter what we have. We've talked together about generosity, and we've seen that we can never have the life we want most—a life of joy—until we learn to give the gift of generosity.

Generosity changes us. We were created to be generous, and our generosity can be a great blessing in our lives. I pray that through your giving, you will find that blessings flow back into your life—blessings that you're not expecting and that surprise you. I pray that you will find that your generosity changes the world as it changes one person at a time. This is my prayer for you—and for our entire congregation.

My hope is that you will find yourself blessed as you experience joy in your generosity. Again, thank you for all that you do to make possible the ministry of our church. You make a difference here!

In Christ,

They are to do good, to be rich in good works, generous, and ready to share, thus storing up for themselves the treasure of a good foundation for the future, so that they may take hold of the life that really is life.

(1 Timothy 6:18-19)

MAILING 5B

RESPONDING MEMBERS BOOKMARK*

[Side One: Can be art, a Bible verse, or your church name and address. In this example found in your download, a verse from the Shaker song "Simple Gifts" is used.]

> *'Tis the gift to be simple, 'tis the gift to be free . . .*
> *—19th-century Shaker song*

[Side Two]

Thank you

Thank you for sharing your estimate of giving with our church this year. Your gifts are an act of worship and an investment in opportunities for God to work through us. Our prayer is that you will find greater contentment and simplicity in your life as you put God first in your giving and living and that you will experience the joy that comes from knowing that our gifts honor God and change lives.

---

*Note: if you choose to provide a bookmark as part of this mailing, the bookmark will need to be designed and printed in advance. Make sure to allocate sufficient time for the bookmark to be designed and produced before this mailing. Artwork that can be used in the design of the bookmark can be found in the download in the Art Resources folder.

Enough: Stewardship Program Guide

MAILING 5C

NONRESPONDING MEMBERS / WITH RETURN ENVELOPE

Valued Member Survey

The purpose of this survey is to identify additional needs of the members of [church name]. We ask for your help with this important aspect of our ministry. Please check the correct answer to questions 1–3, and check all the relevant answers to question 4.

1. Are you currently a member of [church name]?
   - ❏ Yes
   - ❏ No

2. How many church services have you attended in the last thirteen weeks?
   - ❏ 6 or more
   - ❏ 3–5
   - ❏ 1–2
   - ❏ None

3. In what groups at [church name] are you active?
   - ❏ Adult Sunday school
   - ❏ Small group
   - ❏ Disciple Bible Study
   - ❏ Choir
   - ❏ Not active in a group
   - ❏ Other:

4. Please identify the factors that influenced your decision not to return a commitment card for [calendar year]. (Please check all items that influenced your decision.)
   - ❏ My commitment card has been returned
   - ❏ I will continue to offer my financial support this year
   - ❏ Personal financial issues
   - ❏ Health issues
   - ❏ Personal issues in my family

- ❏ Relocating
- ❏ Became unemployed
- ❏ Misplaced the commitment card or forgot
- ❏ Unable to attend worship services
- ❏ Have started attending another church
- ❏ I will complete a commitment card next year
- ❏ Concerns about the church
- ❏ Felt the church did not respond to my needs
- ❏ Did not feel a part of the church
- ❏ Did not feel that my commitment was needed

Thank you for taking the time to share this information. Please return this survey by [date] using the enclosed postage-paid envelope, or place it in the offering plate in a worship service. Please do not sign this anonymous survey unless you wish to update your membership records or desire a call from a minister of our church. Survey results will help us better serve the congregation.

[Pastor's name and/or committee name]

E-MAIL FROM PASTOR 1

Our churchwide emphasis *Enough: Discovering Joy Through Simplicity and Generosity* is in full swing! Last Sunday our topic was "When Dreams Become Nightmares." We saw how the American Dream contrasts with God's vision, and how God's vision brings joy that the American Dream never can. If you were unable to be with us, you can find the sermon message on our website, [website address].

This Sunday our topic will be "Wisdom and Finance." We will look closely at the biblical principles of money management and discover how they apply to our daily lives. I invite you to join us for this extremely informative and practical message. You also will receive several tools that will help you in your own financial planning. See you on Sunday!

E-MAIL FROM PASTOR 2

We are halfway through our churchwide emphasis *Enough: Discovering Joy Through Simplicity and Generosity*. Last Sunday our topic was "Wisdom and Finance." We looked closely at the biblical principles of money management and learned how they apply to our daily lives. We also reviewed some common pitfalls and cultural traps and discovered how we can avoid them. If you were unable to be with us, you can find the sermon message and two financial planning worksheets on our website, [website address].

This Sunday our topic will be "Cultivating Contentment." If you ever feel a strong desire to have more, or if you ever look at your surroundings and feel overwhelmed by the sheer volume of things, then you don't want to miss this message! We will address head-on our human tendency to accumulate possessions and wealth and will learn how to change our ways. We also will be handing out a special tool that will help us refocus daily on contentment and simplicity. I hope you will join us!

E-MAIL FROM PASTOR 3

Our churchwide emphasis *Enough: Discovering Joy Through Simplicity and Generosity* is nearing its conclusion. Last week we talked about "Cultivating Contentment." In our small groups and our corporate worship, we addressed head-on our human tendency to accumulate possessions and wealth, and we discovered how to change our ways. If you were unable to be with us, check out the sermon message on our website, [website address].

This Sunday brings our final topic in the series: "Defined by Generosity." What defines your life? Is it wealth? belongings? faith? Many of us live with a scarcity mentality, worried that we must gather and hoard as much as possible, saving for some imagined "rainy day." Or we focus on self-gratification. But the Bible promises both God's blessings and joy for those who choose to live another way. During the service we will take action to change our lives by setting five specific personal goals to work toward over the next year. Then, on the following two Sundays, we will consecrate our gifts to the ministry of our church for the coming year.

I urge you to join us this Sunday as we learn how to live a new way—as people who are defined by generosity and who experience true joy.

E-MAIL FROM PASTOR 4

Last Sunday concluded our churchwide study and worship emphasis called *Enough: Discovering Joy Through Simplicity and Generosity*. The final topic of our series was "Defined by Generosity." We considered the futility and emptiness of accumulating and hoarding possessions and wealth, and we saw that God promises blessings and joy to those who choose to live a life of generosity and self-sacrifice. We also took action to change our lives by setting five specific personal goals to work toward over the next year. If you were unable to be with us, you can find the sermon message and goals worksheet on our website, [website address].

This week you will be receiving a commitment card, called an Estimate of Giving Commitment Card, in the mail. On a practical level, we ask our members to turn in Estimate of Giving Commitment Cards each year so that our Finance Committee is able to set an accurate ministry budget for the coming year. This allows us to make the most of every dollar given to the church. On a personal level, the commitment card is an opportunity for you to spend time in prayer and reflection, considering what offering you would make to God through our church in the coming year. Please be watching for the mailing. Then fill out the card and bring it with you to worship this week for Consecration Sunday, [date]. We also will have a second Consecration Sunday on [date] to ensure that everyone is able to participate. (If you choose, you can pledge online at [website address].) I hope you will be able to join us for one or both of these meaningful services as we celebrate and consecrate our gifts to the ministry of our church for the coming year.

E-MAIL FROM PASTOR 5

This Sunday we will have another opportunity to consecrate our commitments of giving for the coming year. If you were unable to attend last week's service or did not bring forward your Estimate of Giving Commitment Card for some other reason, I invite you to do so this week. If you have misplaced your commitment card, additional cards will be available in [location]. I hope you will join us for this meaningful time of commitment and celebration. My prayer is that you will come to experience the joy that comes from knowing that your giving honors God and changes lives!

E-MAIL FROM PASTOR 6

These past [number] weeks have been such a meaningful time in the life of our congregation. We have explored how we can manage our financial resources and truly experience simplicity, generosity, and joy. And we have responded to all that we have learned by setting personal goals and making commitments. On the previous two Sundays, we have consecrated our commitments of giving for God's work through our church.

If you have already made your estimate of giving, thank you. If you have not yet had an opportunity to do so, it's not too late. Simply drop your Estimate of Giving Commitment Card in the mail, bring it by the church office, or put it the offering plate during any worship service. If you need another card, extras are available at [location].

We are grateful for your financial support of our church. Your giving in the coming year will make a difference in the lives of children, youth, and adults in our church, as well as in the lives of people everywhere we are in mission and ministry in the world.

BULLETIN INSERT 1

MY LIFE AND FINANCIAL GOALS WORKSHEET

My Life and Financial Goals

How would you define or describe your life purpose?

_____
_____
_____

What are some goals that can help you achieve this life purpose?

_____
_____
_____

What are some financial goals that can help support your life goals and purpose?

_____
_____
_____

Short-term financial goals (next 12 months):

1. _____
2. _____

Mid-range financial goals (2–5 years):

1. _____
2. _____

Long-term financial goals (5 years to retirement):

1. _____
2. _____

Enough: Stewardship Program Guide

BULLETIN INSERT 2
BASIC BUDGET WORKSHEET

Item	Actual %	Suggested %*	Plan for next 12 months
Housing		25–35%	
Transportation		10–15%	
Charitable Gifts		10–12%	
Food		5–15%	
Saving		5–10%	
Utilities		5–10%	
Medical/Health		5–10%	
Debt		5–10%	
Clothing		2–7%	
Miscellaneous		12–23%	

* These percentages are adapted from Dave Ramsey's *The Total Money Makeover* (Thomas Nelson, 2007).

Communication Resources

BULLETIN INSERT 3
COMMITMENT CARD*

[Panel 1]

Enough: Discovering Joy Through Simplicity and Generosity

We thank you for your generous acceptance of stewardship and pray you may find the level of giving that is right for you as you progress in your journey of faith and commitment. Your pledges and contributions are a critical part of how we can make a difference in our church, our community, and our world.

Please complete this Estimate of Giving Commitment Card and return it in the offering plate or to the church office. You may change your commitment at any time by notifying the church office. If you have questions regarding this card, call _____.

Electronic Funds Transfer

Electronic Funds Transfer (EFT) is a convenient and reliable way to fulfill your financial commitment to the church. EFT is also the most cost-efficient method of giving to the church, since it reduces administrative costs and helps maintain a predictable cash flow. To choose EFT, fill in the EFT section on the commitment card.

[Panel 2]

Estimate of Giving

Name (Please Print) _____

Address _____

City/State/Zip _____

E-mail _____

Home Phone _____

Yes! I/We will support the church in the coming year.

Choose one:

$ _____ weekly for 52 weeks

$ _____ semi-monthly for 24 periods

$ _____ monthly for 12 months

$ _____ as follows _____

Signature _____

Date _____

Electronic Funds Transfer Authorization

Please indicate the frequency of the automatic draft.

- ❏ Weekly—Withdrawn on Mondays
- ❏ Semi-Monthly—Withdrawn first and third Monday of each month
- ❏ Monthly—Withdrawn the first Monday of each month
- ❏ Monthly—Withdrawn the third Monday of each month

- ❏ Use bank account information currently on file.

-or-

- ❏ Attach a voided check for the account from which withdrawals will be made.

Withdrawals will begin in January unless otherwise specified.

Note: All withdrawals will be on the indicated day unless it is a non-banking business day, in which case the withdrawal will take place on the next banking business day.

BULLETIN INSERT 4

PERSONAL GOALS AND COMMITMENT

Enough Stewardship Campaign

During the past few weeks, we have examined some of the financial challenges facing us as a nation, and we have looked at our own spending, saving, and giving habits. We have examined the biblical principles of financial management, and we have learned about ways to assess our financial situation and develop a financial plan that will allow us to experience the true joy that comes through simplicity and generosity. Now, on this Consecration Sunday, I ask God's blessing of my commitment to these financial goals for the upcoming year.

My Personal Goals and Commitment for (Next Calendar Year)

1. I will thank God daily for all my blessings.

    My goal for daily Bible reading and prayer is _____ days each week.

2. I will seek contentment and simplicity and live within my means.

    My spending goal is _____.

3. I will seek freedom from the bonds of credit and debt.

    My debt reduction goal is _____.

4. I will seek to wisely manage the gifts God has given me, investing and saving for the future.

    My saving goal is _____.

5. I will worship God each week by the giving of my tithes and offerings.

    My estimate of giving for (<u>next calendar year</u>) is _____.

Lord, I present this commitment to you, acknowledging that everything I have and everything I am is a gift from you. I pray that you will grant me wisdom and strength in the coming year, and that you will bless and use the gifts that I humbly present to you. Amen.

STEWARDSHIP CAMPAIGN FOLLOW-UP

SCRIPT FOR CARING CONTACT CALLS

Caller name: _____

Date: _____

These phone calls are to be made to those who returned an Estimate of Giving Commitment Card for [current calendar year] but have NOT for [next calendar year].

Step 1: Call and offer our concern.

"Hi, this is _____ from [church name]'s stewardship campaign follow-up team.

"We're thankful for your financial and prayerful support of [church name]! We're calling because we received your Estimate of Giving Commitment Card for [current calendar year] last fall but for some reason we haven't received your card for [next calendar year]. [Name], are there any concerns, needs, or questions we might answer at this time?" (List these on back of sheet.)

Step 2: Seek commitment.

"Will you be returning an Estimate of Giving Commitment Card for [next calendar year]? Do you need for us to mail you a card, or would you prefer to fill out a card at church and place it in the offering plate or make your commitment online?"

❏ Mail
❏ Card in offering plate
❏ Online

Step 3: Pray with the people if they are experiencing problems or issues.

"*Lord, I lift up [name] to you. Bless [name] with the strength of your love. We thank you for our church family and pray for opportunities to support and encourage one another. In Christ's name. Amen.*"

Step 4: Express appreciation.

"Thank you for your continued support of our ministries at [church name]. Have a great day!"

Step 5: Evaluate the response to your call.

On a scale of 1–10, with 10 being the best, how well do you think your call was received (from irritated to appreciated)?

Thank you for serving in this telephone ministry!

CHAPTER FOUR

ART RESOURCES

ACCESS THE CAMPAIGN RESOURCES
DOWNLOAD AT:

AbingdonPress.com/Enough

ART RESOURCES FOR PROMOTING YOUR STEWARDSHIP CAMPAIGN

During your campaign, you may want to design some announcements, posters, postcards, letterhead, brochures, or printed materials. In the Campaign Resources accompanying this book, you will find a variety of art and image files that are provided to assist with these needs. Among the high-resolution files included are:

- Book cover images
- Color and grayscale versions of the *Enough* logo
- Art for a 48-inch x 24-inch banner (a graphic that can be used as a background or a PDF that can be edited to include your church's information)
- Letterhead background art
- Letterhead header that can be used to create your own letterhead
- Two letter-size images (11 inches x 8.5 inches) that are higher resolution versions of the images provided as Sermon Helps; these may also be used to create presentation slides.
- Art for an 11-inch x 17-inch poster (a graphic that can be used as a background or a PDF that can be edited to include your church's information)

You will also find a set of lower-resolution art meant to be used for your church's websites and social media. Included in the download are:

- Book cover images
- Color and grayscale versions of the *Enough* logo
- Web banner images (1280 pixels x 320 pixels, which match the Letterhead Header image)

On the following pages, you will find some reduced-size examples of the art included in the download.

Front Cover Art

Logo
Print and web versions available in color or grayscale.

Art Resources

Banner (48 inches x 24 inches)
Available as an editable PDF or as a background graphic to create your own.

Poster (11 inches x 17 inches)
Available as an editable PDF or as a background graphic to create your own.

Version 1

Version 2

Letter-size Images (11 inches x 8.5 inches)

Art is a higher resolution version of the files provided as Presentation Images in the Sermon Helps folder in the download. It can be used for a variety of purposes.

Art Resources

Letterhead (8.5 inches x 11 inches)
Available as a PDF or JPEG image.
Files include bleed on all edges to make the full art size 8.75 inches x 11.25 inches.

Letterhead Header (8 inches x 2 inches) / Web Banner (1280 pixels x 320 pixels)
Letterhead header is available as a PDF or JPEG.
It can be placed in your own document to create a letterhead for the stewardship campaign.

Web banner is available as a JPEG or PNG file.
It can be used for a variety of purposes on the web.

CHAPTER FIVE

WORSHIP HELPS

SERMON OUTLINE 1

"WHEN DREAMS BECOME NIGHTMARES"

> *Some people, eager for money, have wandered from the faith and pierced themselves with many griefs.*
>
> *(1 Timothy 6:10b NIV)*
>
> *The lover of money will not be satisfied with money; nor the lover of wealth, with gain. This also is vanity.*
>
> *(Ecclesiastes 5:10)*
>
> *"For what will it profit them if they gain the whole world but forfeit their life? Or what will they give in return for their life?"*
> *(Matthew 16:26)*

The American Dream

What characterizes the greatest hopes, desires, and dreams of most Americans?

For most people, the American Dream has to do with a desire for achieving success and satisfying the desire for material possessions. It is the opportunity to pursue more than what we have, to gain more than what we have, and to meet success. We tend to measure our success by the stuff that we possess.

The pursuit of immediate material pleasure

The love of money and the things money can buy is a primary or secondary motive behind most of what we Americans do. We want to consume, acquire, and buy our way to happiness—and we want it now.

The American Nightmare

The American Dream has become an American Nightmare owing to two distinct yet related "illnesses" that affect us both socially and spiritually.

Affluenza

"Affluenza" is the constant need for more and bigger and better stuff—as well as the effect that this need has on us. It is the desire to acquire, and most of us have been infected by this virus to some degree.

- The average American home went from 1,660 square feet in 1973 to 2,700 square feet in 2016.[1]
- Today there is estimated to be 2.3 billion square feet of self-storage space in America.[2]

Credit-itis

"Credit-itis" is an illness that is brought on by the opportunity to buy now and pay later, and it feeds on our desire for instant gratification. Our economy today is built on the concept of credit-itis. Unfortunately, it has exploited our lack of self-discipline and has allowed us to feed our affluenza, wreaking havoc with our personal and national finances.

- Average credit card debt in America in 1990 was around $3,000. Today it's nearly $17,000.[3]
- The average sale is around 125 percent higher if we use a credit card than if we pay cash, because it doesn't feel real when we use plastic instead of cash.
- Credit-itis is not limited to purchases made with credit cards; it extends to car loans, mortgages, and other loans. The life of the average car loan and home mortgage continues to increase, while the average American's savings rate continues to decline.

The Deeper Problem Within

There is a spiritual issue behind both affluenza and credit-itis.

Our souls were created in the image of God, but they have been distorted. We were meant to desire God, but we have turned that desire toward possessions. We were meant to find our security in God, but we find it in amassing wealth. We were meant to love people, but instead we compete with them. We were meant to enjoy the simple pleasures of life, but we busy ourselves with pursuing money and things. We were meant to be generous and to share with those in need, but we selfishly hoard our resources for ourselves. All of us have an inclination toward sin.

The devil plays upon this inclination toward sin.

Jesus said, "The thief comes only to steal and kill and destroy. I came that they may have life, and

---

[1] www.aei.org/publication/new-us-homes-today-are-1000-square-feet-larger-than-in-1973-and-living-space-per-person-has-nearly-doubled/

[2] www.statisticbrain.com/self-storage-industry-statistics/

[3] www.nerdwallet.com/blog/average-credit-card-debt-household/

have it abundantly" (John 10:10). In order to destroy us, the devil doesn't need to tempt us to do drugs or to steal or to have an extramarital affair. All he needs to do is convince us to keep pursuing the American Dream—to keep up with the Joneses, borrow against our futures, enjoy more than we can afford, and indulge ourselves. By doing that, the devil will rob us of joy, make us slaves, and keep us from doing God's will.

- Matthew 4:8-10
- Luke 8:14
- Mark 8:36
- 1 Timothy 6:10

The Bible's Solution

We need a heart change.

Although we receive a changed heart when we accept Christ, in a sense we need a heart change every morning. Each morning we should get down on our knees and say, "Lord, help me to be the person you want me to be today. Take away the desires that shouldn't be there, and help me to be single-minded in my focus and pursuit of you." As we say this prayer and act on it, God comes and cleanses us from the inside out, purifying and changing our hearts.

We must allow Christ to work in us.

Christ works in us as we first seek his kingdom and strive to do his will. As we do, we begin to sense a higher calling—a calling to simplicity and faithfulness and generosity. We begin to look at ways we can make a difference with our time and talents and resources. By pursuing good financial practices, we free ourselves from debt so that we are able to be in mission to the world. A key part of finding financial and spiritual freedom is found in simplicity and in exercising restraint. With the help of God, we can

- simplify our lives and silence the voices constantly telling us we need more.
- live counterculturally by living below, not above, our means.
- build into our budgets the money to buy with cash instead of credit.
- build into our budgets what we need to live generously and faithfully.

Closing Prayer

I'd like to invite you to put your hands on your lap—just extend your hands palm upright on your lap. And I would invite you to say this prayer with me, quietly under your breath.

Change my heart, O God. Clean me out inside. Make me new. Heal my desires. Help me to hold my possessions loosely. Help me to love you. Teach me simplicity. Teach me generosity and help me have joy. I offer my life to you. In Jesus' name. Amen.

SERMON OUTLINE 2

"WISDOM AND FINANCE"

*The plans of the diligent lead surely to abundance,
but everyone who is hasty comes only to want.*

(Proverbs 21:5)

*Precious treasure remains in the house of the wise,
but the fool devours it.*

(Proverbs 21:20)

Where Did All Our Money Go?

Living as prodigals

From Jesus' description in Luke 15:11-16, we see that the prodigal son had the habits of squandering and spending. The word prodigal does not mean someone who wanders away or is lost. It literally means "one who wastes money." Many of us struggle with that habit. We're not worried about tomorrow; we want it today. The problem with that kind of thinking is that, for most of us, the "famine" eventually comes. It comes when we have spent everything we have and even a little bit of next year's income. So we use the credit card and charge it, and we go a little further into debt. Finally, we come to a place where we have nothing left, not even credit, and we can't figure out how we are we going to get by.

The more we make, the more we waste.

It seems that the more financially secure we become, the less we worry about spending money here and there. We waste a dollar on this or that, and we forget where it went. Money just seems to flow through our fingers. We're not as careful with our money as we should be. There are many ways we waste money, but there are two primary money-wasters that many of us struggle with. It is not necessary to eliminate these two things altogether, but we should think more carefully about how we spend our money.

How to avoid impulse buying

- Never go grocery shopping when you are hungry.
- Shop only for what you need.
- Make a list and stick to it; buy what you need and get out of the store!
- Wait twenty-four hours before following through on an impulse buy.

Eating out

- The issue is frequency. The average American eats out an average of four times a week.
- By eating out less frequently, we will have more money to save, to spend on more important things, and to give away.

Clarifying Our Relationship with Money and Possessions

We do not exist simply to consume as much as we can and get as much pleasure as we can while we are here on this earth. We have a higher purpose. We need to know and understand our life purpose—our vision or mission or calling—and then spend our money in ways that are consistent with this purpose or calling.

Be clear about your purpose and calling.

Our society tells us that our life purpose is to consume—to make as much money as possible and then to spend it. The Bible tells us that we were created to care for God's creation. We were created to love God and to love our neighbors as ourselves. We were created to care for our families and those in need. We were created to glorify God, to seek justice, and to do mercy. Our money and possessions should be devoted to helping us fulfill this calling. We are to use our resources to help care for our families and others—to serve Christ and the world through the church, missions, and everyday opportunities. We have a life purpose that is greater than our own self-interest, and how we spend our God-given resources reflects our understanding and commitment to this life purpose or mission.

Set worthy goals.

Being able to accomplish the greater purposes God has for our lives requires some measure of planning. Taking the time to set goals related to our lives and our finances is crucial if we are to become wise stewards of our God-given resources. Each of us should think about our life purpose and goals and then identify two short-term financial goals, two mid-range financial goals, and two long-term financial goals that are aimed at helping us accomplish our broader life goals. At least one goal in each category should relate specifically to our faith. (Suggestion: Use the bulletin insert "My Life and Financial Goals Worksheet" in 3. Communication Resources.)

The Discipline of Managing Your Money

Adopt a budget and spending plan.

Once we've set some financial goals, we need to develop a plan to meet those goals. A budget is a spending plan that enables us to accomplish our goals. Some people use an envelope system to help them manage their saving and spending and stay on budget. Others use a variety of different approaches. Many people find it helpful to seek the advice of a financial advisor. For those who find themselves in the midst of a financial crisis, a financial counselor can help arrange terms with creditors and develop a workable financial plan. Whatever approach you choose, the important thing is simply to have a plan.

Follow six financial planning principles.

The following financial planning principles can help us manage our money with wisdom and faith:

1. **Pay your tithe and offering first.**
   Put God first in your living and your giving. Give your tithe and offering from the "top" of your paycheck, and then live on whatever remains.

2. **Create a budget and track your expenses.**
   Creating a budget is simply developing a plan in which you tell your money what you want it to do. Tracking your expenses with a budget is like getting on the scales: it allows you to see how you are doing and motivates you to be more careful with your expenditures. (*Suggestion: Use the bulletin insert "Basic Budget Worksheet."*)

3. **Simplify your lifestyle (live below your means).**
   Because this discipline is critical to the success of any financial plan, next Sunday's sermon will be devoted to this topic.

4. **Establish an emergency fund.**
   An emergency fund is an account separate from checking or long-term savings that is set aside specifically for emergencies. Financial advisor Dave Ramsey recommends beginning with $1,000 and building that to three months' worth of income.[1] When you have this amount, you won't need to use your credit cards anymore.

5. **Pay off your credit cards, use debit cards for purchases, and use credit wisely.**
   As you are building your emergency fund, begin to pay off your credit card debt and start using cash or debit cards for purchases. Some experts suggest starting with the credit card that has the highest interest rate. Others suggest paying down the smallest debt first, experiencing that victory, and applying your payments from the first card to the second, and so on, creating a snowball effect to pay off the cards as soon as possible. Cut up your cards as you pay them down so that you are not trapped or leveraged by your future for present-day pleasure, as the prodigal son was. If you must use a credit card, such as when traveling or making purchases online, be sure to pay off the debt monthly. If you are unable to do this, then it is better for you to cut up your cards and stop using them altogether.

---

[1] Dave Ramsey, *The Total Money Makeover: A Proven Plan for Financial Fitness* (Nashville: Thomas Nelson, 2007), 102–108.

6. **Practice long-term savings and investing habits.**
    Saving money is the number-one wise money management principle everyone should practice. We do not save merely for the sake of saving. There is a word for that: *hoarding*. Hoarding is frowned upon in the Bible as the practice of fools and those who fail to understand the purpose of life. Saving, on the other hand, is meant to be purposeful. There are three types of savings we should have: for emergencies, for wants and goals, and for retirement.

Closing Prayer

God, you know all about us, even when we don't. We don't know where every dime went, but somehow you know what we did with all that we had, last year and every other year. You don't forbid us from having joy in our possessions; in fact, you delight in our having joy. But what you know is that simply acquiring more stuff isn't where we find joy. Lord, forgive us for being wasteful, for being prodigal. Forgive us for leveraging our future in order to have pleasure in the present. And help us to be good managers of the talents that you've given us. Help us to be generous and willing to share, kingdom-minded and focused on accomplishing your purposes for our lives. In Jesus' name. Amen.

SERMON OUTLINE 3
"CULTIVATING CONTENTMENT"

Keep your lives free from the love of money, and be content with what you have; for he has said, "I will never leave you or forsake you." So we can say with confidence,

> *"The Lord is my helper;*
> *I will not be afraid.*
> *What can anyone do to me?"*

(Hebrews 13:5-6)

[Jesus] said to them, "Take care! Be on your guard against all kinds of greed; for one's life does not consist in the abundance of possessions."

(Luke 12:15)

Whatever my eyes desired I did not keep from them; I kept my heart from no pleasure. . . . Then I considered all that my hands had done and the toil I had spent in doing it, and again, all was vanity and a chasing after wind.

(Ecclesiastes 2:10-11)

In recent years we have witnessed a number of devastating natural disasters, including hurricanes, floods, tornadoes, and wildfires. Natural disasters remind us that everything in this world is temporary. This is why we can say with Jesus, "[My] life does not consist in the abundance of possessions" (Luke 12:15). Yet the culture is shouting that it's not true. The result is a wrestling match in our hearts. Despite the fact that we say we believe Jesus' words, we still find ourselves devoting a great deal of our time, talents, and resources to the acquisition of more stuff. We say that our lives do not consist in the abundance of our possessions, but we live as if they do.

Restless Heart Syndrome: Struggling with Discontent

Perhaps you've heard of restless legs syndrome (RLS), a condition in which one has twitches and contractions in the legs. Something I call Restless Heart Syndrome (RHS) works in a similar way, but in the heart—or soul. Its primary symptom is discontent. We find that we are never satisfied with anything. The moment we acquire something, we scarcely take time to enjoy it before we want something else. We are perennially discontent.

When discontent is a virtue

There is a certain discontent that God intended us to have. God actually wired our hearts so that we would not be content with certain things, causing us to seek the only One who can fully satisfy us. We are meant to yearn for a relationship with God, to cultivate a deeper prayer life, to pursue justice and holiness with increasing fervor, to love others more, and to grow in grace and character and wisdom with each passing day.

When discontent destroys

The problem is that those things we should be content with are the very things we find ourselves hopelessly discontented with. For example, we find ourselves discontented with our stuff, our jobs, our churches, our children, and our spouses. God must look down on us and feel the way we feel when we give someone a special gift and the person asks for the gift receipt. It's as if we're saying to God, "I don't like what you have given me, God. I want to trade it in and get something better."

Four Keys to Cultivating Contentment

The Apostle Paul is an excellent example of contentment. In his letter to the Philippians, he wrote about the "secret" of his contentment (Philippians 4:11-12). Like Paul, we can learn to be content in whatever circumstances we may find ourselves. Four keys, which include the "secret" Paul referred to in his letter, can help us to do that.

1. **Four words to repeat: It could be worse.**
   John Ortberg, pastor at Menlo Park Presbyterian Church in California, says there are four words we should say whenever we find ourselves discontented with something or someone: "It could be worse." This is essentially the practice of looking on the bright side or finding the silver lining. It is recognizing that no matter what we may not like about a thing or person or circumstance, we can always find something good to focus on if only we will choose to do so.

2. **One question to ask: How long will this make me happy?**
   So often we buy something, thinking it will make us happy, only to find that the happiness lasts about as long as it takes to open the box. There is a moment of satisfaction when we make the purchase, but the item does not continue to bring satisfaction over a period of time. Many of the things we buy are simply not worth the expense. This is why it is a good idea to try before you buy.

3. **Develop a grateful heart.**
   Gratitude is essential if we are to be content. The Apostle Paul said that we are to "give thanks in all circumstances" (1 Thessalonians 5:18). A grateful heart recognizes that all of life is a gift. Contentment comes when we spend more time giving thanks for what we have than thinking about what's missing or wrong in our lives.

4. **Where does your soul find true satisfaction?**
   The world tells us that we find satisfaction in ease and luxury and comfort and money. The Bible, however, answers this question very differently. From Genesis to Revelation, it tells us that we find our satisfaction in God alone.

   - "Thou hast made us for thyself, O Lord, and our hearts are restless until they find their rest in thee." (Saint Augustine)
   - "O God, you are my God, I seek you, / my soul thirsts for you. . . . / My soul is satisfied as with a rich feast, / and my mouth praises you with joyful lips / when I think of you on my bed, / and meditate on you in the watches of the night." (Psalm 63:1, 5-6)
   - "Whatever my eyes desired I did not keep from them; I kept my heart from no pleasure. . . . Then I considered all that my hands had done and the toil I had spent in doing it, and again, all was vanity and a chasing after wind." (Ecclesiastes 2:10-11)
   - Jesus said the two most important things we must do are to "love the Lord your God with all your heart, and with all your soul, and with all your mind," and to "love your neighbor as yourself" (Matthew 22:37, 39). If we keep our focus on these two things, we will find satisfaction for our souls and lasting contentment.

Five Steps for Simplifying Our Lives

In addition to cultivating contentment in our lives, we need simplicity. Contentment and simplicity go hand in hand.

1. **Set a goal of reducing your consumption, and live below your means.**
   Set a tangible goal to reduce your own personal consumption and the production of waste in your life. For example, use canvas bags when you go grocery shopping and refuse any extra packaging. Whenever you are making purchases, look at the mid-grade instead of the top-of-the-line product. When buying a new car, aim to improve fuel economy over your existing car by at least 10 percent. Reduce your utilities 10 percent by setting the thermostat back a couple of degrees when you are away during the day and asleep at night. Find other ways to reduce your consumption and live below your means. To find other ways of reducing consumption, do some research, share ideas with others, or have a brainstorming session with your family.

2. **Before making a purchase, ask yourself: Do I really need this? Why do I want this?**
   These questions will help you determine the true motivation for your desired purchase. Is it a need, a self-esteem issue, or something else? You may find yourself wrestling with your true motive and decide that your reason for purchasing the item is not a good one.

3. **Use something up before buying something new.**
   Take good care of the things you buy and use them until they are empty, broken, or worn out. Buy things that are made to last, and when buying things that have a short lifespan, spend your money wisely.

4. **Plan low-cost entertainment that enriches.**
   When it comes to choosing entertainment for your family or friends, plan things that are simple and cheap. You'll be amazed at how much more pleasure you derive from low-cost, simple activities.

5. **Ask yourself: Are there major changes that would allow me to simplify my life?**
   Consider downsizing your home, canceling a club membership you don't use, or selling a car to buy one you can pay for in full. Ask yourself questions related to your home, possessions, job, and activities to identify some significant changes that will simplify your life. Remember, if you cannot do all the things God is calling you to do and you're unable to find joy in your life, perhaps it's time to simplify in some major ways.

The Power of Self-Control

Simplifying your life requires the practice of self-control. Solomon wrote, "Like a city whose walls are broken through / is a person who lacks self-control" (Proverbs 25:28 NIV). When a city's walls are broken through, the enemy can march right in and destroy it; there is no longer any protection. Likewise, self-control is a wall around your heart and life that protects you from yourself, from temptation, and from sins that are deadly and ultimately can destroy you. Self-control often comes down to making a choice between instant gratification and delayed gratification for some greater cause. The choice can be examined using three questions:

- What are the long-term consequences of this action?
- Is there a higher good or a better outcome if I use this resource of time, money, or energy in another way?
- Will this action honor God?

Conclusion: Which tent will you live in?

Will you live in "discon-tent" or "con-tent-ment"? You and you alone determine which "tent" will be yours. You choose it in large part by deciding what life is about. If you decide that "life does not consist in the abundance of possessions" (Luke 12:15), then you are choosing contentment. Choosing contentment means we look to God as our Source, giving thanks for what we have; we ask God to give us the right perspective on money and possessions and to change our hearts each day; we decide to live simpler lives, wasting less and conserving more; and we choose to give more generously.

Closing Prayer

Lord, we pray that you might cure us of Restless Heart Syndrome. We are truly sorry for the times when we received the gifts you give us and asked for the gift receipt: when we were dissatisfied with a person you entrusted to our care, with our children or parents, with our home or our car, with our healthcare or our jobs. God forgive us for the times we've offended you by our discontent. Forgive us for being content with the things we should not be content with. Give us a hunger to pursue righteousness and holiness and justice and love, to long for you and for your will in our lives. Help us to simplify, to get off the treadmill, and to find our peace in you. We ask these mercies in your holy name. Amen.

SERMON OUTLINE 4
"DEFINED BY GENEROSITY"

As for those who in the present age are rich, command them not to be haughty, or to set their hopes on the uncertainty of riches, but rather on God who richly provides us with everything for our enjoyment. They are to do good, to be rich in good works, generous, and ready to share, thus storing up for themselves the treasure of a good foundation for the future, so that they may take hold of the life that really is life.
(1 Timothy 6:17-19)

Some give freely, yet grow all the richer;
    others withhold what is due, and only suffer want.
A generous person will be enriched,
    and one who gives water will get water.
(Proverbs 11:24-25)

Those who are generous are blessed,
    for they share their bread with the poor.
(Proverbs 22:9)

A Theological Foundation for a Generous Life

Created to be generous, tempted to hoard

God created us with the willingness to give—to God and to others. This design is part of our makeup; we actually have the need to be generous. Yet there are two voices that work against our God-given impulse toward generosity and that tempt us to keep or hoard what we have.

- The voice of fear
  Fear of what might happen to us, along with a misplaced idea about the true source of our security, keeps us from being generous and leads us to hoard what we have. The truth is that hoarding offers us no real security in this world.

- The voice of self-gratification
  Our culture tells us that our lives consist in the abundance of our possessions and pleasurable experiences. So we find ourselves thinking, *If I give, there won't be enough left for me.*

Defeating the voices

When we give our lives to Christ, invite him to be Lord, and allow the Holy Spirit to begin changing us from the inside out, we find that our fears begin to dissipate and our aim in life shifts from seeking personal pleasure to pleasing God and caring for others. Although we still may wrestle with the voices from time to time, we are able to silence them more readily and effectively the more we grow in Christ. And the more we grow in Christ, realizing that our lives belong to him, the more generous we become. Generosity is a fruit of spiritual growth.

Biblical reasons to give to God and others

- "It is more blessed to give than to receive" (Acts 20:35).
- "Those who want to save their life will lose it, and those who lose their life for my sake will find it" (Matthew 16:25).
- "The earth is the Lord's and all that is in it" (Psalm 24:1).

Biblical guidelines for giving

From the early days of the Old Testament, God's people observed the practice of giving some portion of the best they had to God. A gift offered to God was called the first fruits or the *tithe*, and it equaled one-tenth of one's flocks or crops or income. Abraham was the first to give a tithe or tenth.

- Genesis 14:20b
- Genesis 28:18-22
- Leviticus 27:30-33

Giving a tithe

As Christians who live under the new covenant, we are not bound by the law of Moses; we look to it as a guide. Yet most Christians agree that the tithe is a good guideline for our lives, and one that is pleasing to God. Though tithing can be a struggle, it is possible at virtually every income level. If you cannot tithe right away, take a step in that direction. Perhaps you can give 2 percent or 5 percent or 7 percent. God understands where you are and will help you make the adjustments necessary to become more generous.

Giving beyond the tithe

Tithing is a floor, not a ceiling. God calls us to grow beyond the tithe. We should strive to set aside an additional percentage of our income as offerings for other things that are important to us, such as mission projects, schools, church building funds, and nonprofit organizations.

What Our Giving Means to God

How does our giving affect God?

From the earliest biblical times, the primary way people worshiped God was by building an altar and offering the fruit of their labors upon it to God. They would burn the sacrifice of an animal or grain as a way of expressing their gratitude, devotion, and desire to honor God. The scent of the offering was said to be pleasing to God. It wasn't that God loved the smell of burnt meat and grain. Rather, God saw that people were giving a gift that expressed love, faith, and the desire to please and honor God, and this moved God's heart. When given in this spirit, our offerings bless the Lord.

What is God's response to our giving?
- Luke 6:38
- Matthew 25:14-30

What Our Giving Means to Us

Through it our hearts are changed.

When we are generous—to God and to our families, friends, neighbors, and others who are in need—our hearts are filled with joy. They are enlarged by the very act of giving. When we give generously, we become more generous.

In it we find the blessings of God.

Many Christians have it wrong. They say that if you give, then God will give more back to you. But that is not how it works. We do not give to God so that we can get something in return. The amazing thing is that when we give to God and to others, the blessings just seem to come back to us. Of course, there is no guarantee that if we tithe, we will never lose our job or never have other bad things happen to us. Nevertheless, when we give generously, the unmistakable blessings of God flow into our lives. (*Suggestion: Insert the Personal Goals and Commitment Card in the bulletin and use it at the end of the sermon. Have a time of silent meditation and prayer, inviting everyone to complete a card at this time.*)

Closing Prayer

O God, we thank you that you have given us life, that you sustain us by the power of your Holy Spirit, and that you gave Jesus Christ as an offering for us and for our sins. We thank you for the abundance that we have in our lives. And we pray, O Lord, that you would help us. Help us to honor you with our tithes. Help us to care for the poor and those who are in need. Help us to recognize that it is more blessed to give than to receive. We offer ourselves to you. Guide us now as we prepare to fill out our commitment cards. Help us, O Lord, to do your will. Lead us, we pray. In your holy name. Amen.

WORSHIP VIDEO TEXT

1. When Dreams Become Nightmares
What does success mean to me?
Does it involve money?

In my life, has the American Dream become the American Nightmare?

Do I suffer from Affluenza?
Do I have Credit-itis?

Money problems are spiritual problems.

Jesus said, "I came that they may have life, and have it abundantly." (John 10:10)

I need a heart change.
Every morning.
Every day.

Where do I start?

2. Wisdom and Finance
What is my life purpose?
What is my mission?

What are my daily goals?

What do I spend my money on?

Do I waste my money?
Do I manage my money?

What is a budget?
How do I make a budget and keep it?

A bank at the corner of Wisdom and Faith.

Lord, help me.

3. Cultivating Contentment
There's a wrestling match in my heart.
The world pushes. God pulls.

I never seem satisfied.
I have RHS: Restless Heart Syndrome.

Where does my soul find true satisfaction?

Jesus said, "One's life does not consist in the abundance of possessions." (Luke 12:15)

What does my life consist of?
What can I do?

Give thanks.
Ask God.

4. Defined by Generosity
What was I created for?

I want to be generous, but…

Why am I weak?
Why am I afraid?

"Those who want to save their life will lose it, and those who lose their life for my sake will find it." (Matthew 16:25)

What's a tithe?

Why do I give?

I give to fill my heart.

CHAPTER SIX

SMALL GROUP STUDY

INVOLVING THE CONGREGATION IN STUDY

One of the best ways to take the *Enough* Stewardship Campaign beyond an annual stewardship drive to a transformational experience resulting in spiritual growth and financial health—on both a personal and congregational level—is through small group study. Encourage Sunday school classes, as well as Wednesday night groups and other groups that meet during the week, to read and study the *Enough* program during the campaign emphasis.

This four-week study includes the book, DVD, and leader guide. Using the leader guide, the leader will engage participants in group discussion and walk them through both group and personal application exercises. The study is made up of four sessions, based on the four book chapters and four corresponding videos. (In worship, your congregation may also have four sermons on these topics.)

1. "When Dreams Become Nightmares"
2. "Wisdom and Finance"
3. "Cultivating Contentment"
4. "Defined by Generosity"

Together in group study, class members will have the opportunity for more in-depth study on each of these topics. They will gain greater understanding of core concepts and will establish a support system and accountability group for the weeks ahead, as they implement the spiritual and financial principles and strategies outlined in the study and campaign.

In an ideal program, each adult class and each household would read together the book *Enough* during the emphasis. A deep personal exploration of the study themes, in community and individually, can produce long-range, life-changing transformation.

OVERVIEW OF SMALL GROUP STUDY
(EXCERPT FROM LEADER GUIDE)

Enough is a book-and-video-based study that explores what the Bible teaches us about financial management. Its purpose is to help participants get off the consumerism treadmill and find the joy and contentment that come with a simpler and more generous way of living. Participants will assess their financial situation and develop a financial plan that has a biblical foundation. This four-week study is appropriate for Sunday school classes, study groups, and others desiring to become wise stewards of the resources God has given them. As group leader, your role will be to facilitate the weekly sessions using the book *Enough*, the DVD, and this Leader Guide.

A Quick Overview

Because no two groups are alike, the leader guide for *Enough* is designed to give you flexibility and choice in tailoring the sessions for your group. You may choose one of the following format options, or adapt these as you wish to meet the schedule and needs of your particular group. (*Note:* The times indicated in parentheses are merely estimates. You may move at a faster or slower pace, making adjustments as necessary to stay on schedule.)

Basic Option: 60 minutes
Opening Prayer (2 minutes)
Biblical Foundation (3 minutes)
Video Presentation (15–20 minutes)
Group Discussion (25–30 minutes)
Taking It to Heart This Week (5 minutes)
Closing Prayer (<5 minutes)

Extended Option: 90 minutes
Opening Prayer (2 minutes)
Biblical Foundation (3 minutes)
Opening Activity (10–15 minutes)
Video Presentation (15–20 minutes)

Group Discussion (25–30 minutes)
Group Activity (15 minutes)
Taking It to Heart This Week (5 minutes)
Closing Prayer (<5 minutes)

Although you are encouraged to adapt the sessions to meet your needs, you also are encouraged to make prayer and Scripture regular components of the weekly group sessions. Feel free to use the opening and closing prayers provided or create your own prayers. In either case, the intent is to "cover" the group session in prayer, acknowledging that we are incapable of becoming wise stewards of our resources apart from God's grace and help. Likewise, the Scripture verses provided for each group session are intended to provide a biblical foundation for the group session as well as for participants' continuing reflection and application during the week.

In addition to the session elements listed above, the following leader helps are provided to equip you for each group session:

- Main Idea (session theme)
- Session Goals (objectives for the group session)
- Key Insights (summary of main points from the video)
- Leader Extra (additional information related to the topic)
- Notable Quote (noteworthy quote from the video)

You may use these helps for your personal preparation only, or you may choose to incorporate them into the group session in some way. For example, you might choose to write the main idea and/or session goals on a board or chart prior to the beginning of class, review the key insights from the video either before or after group discussion, incorporate the leader extra into group discussion, and close with the notable quote.

In addition to the materials provided for each group session, you will find a reproducible participant handout at the end of each session. This handout includes a summary of the key insights from the video as well as "Taking It to Heart This Week" application exercises for the coming week. Remind participants that these exercises are designed to help them get the most out of this study that they possibly can. They alone are the ones who will determine whether this is just another group study or a transformational experience that will have a lasting, positive impact on their lives.